FOLLOW @RICKYTHEUNICORN ON INSTAGRAM FOR MORE DESIGNS!

HOW TO USE THE STENCILS?

1.  CARVE OUT A CIRCLE AROUND THE STEM AND CLEAN OUT THE INSIDE WITH A SPOON

2.  CUT OUT THE PAGE THAT YOU LIKE THE MOST

3.  TAPE IT TO THE PUMPKIN AND TRACE THE IMAGE WITH A PENCIL

4.  CAREFULLY CUT OUT THE SHAPES WITH A KNIFE

5.  PLACE A CANDLE INSIDE THE PUMPKIN AND ENJOY IT!

SCARY FACE

TRICK OR TREAT

TRICK OR TREAT

SPOOKY BATS

SPOOKY FACE

CAULDRON

FUNNY FACE

CUTE GHOST

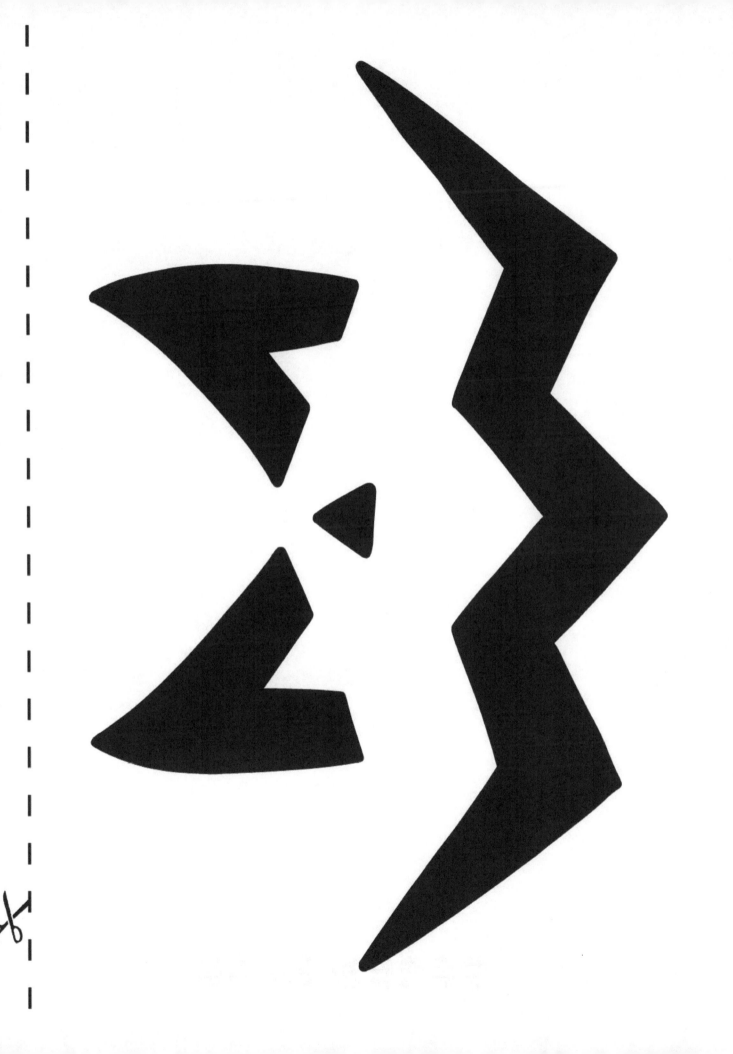

SCARY FACE

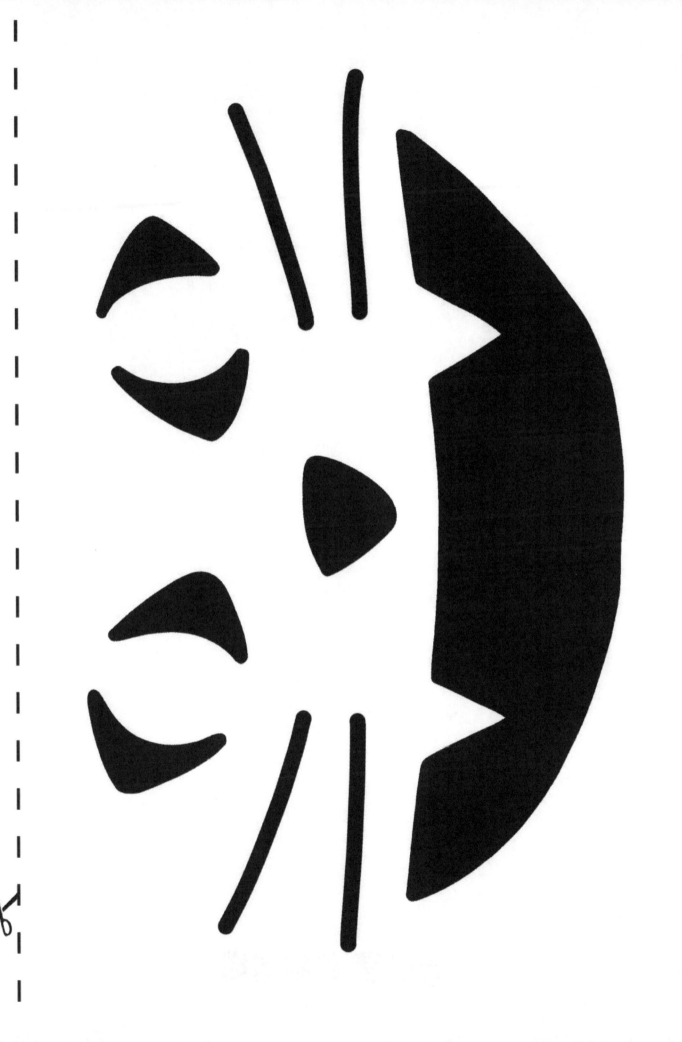

CAT FACE

I LOVE YOU

LOVELY FACE

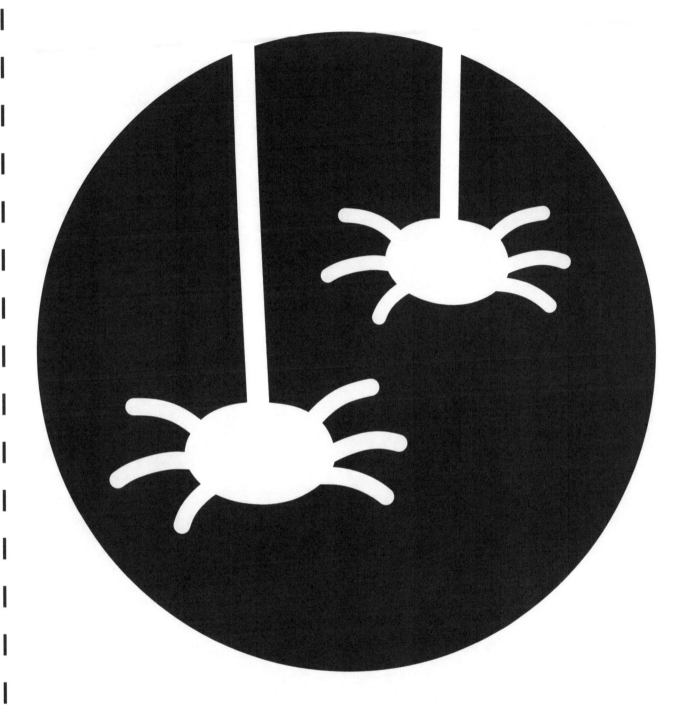

CUTE SPIDERS

FUNNY FACE

WITCHY HAT

FUNNY FACE

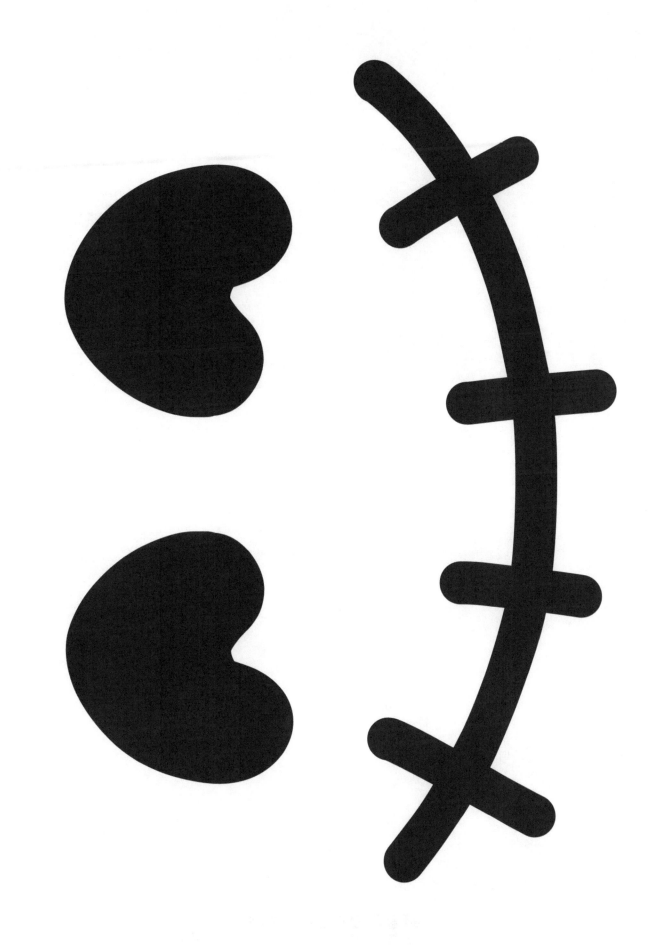

CUTE FACE

MOON AND STARS

SPOOKY FACE

SPOOKY BATS

MAGIC HAT

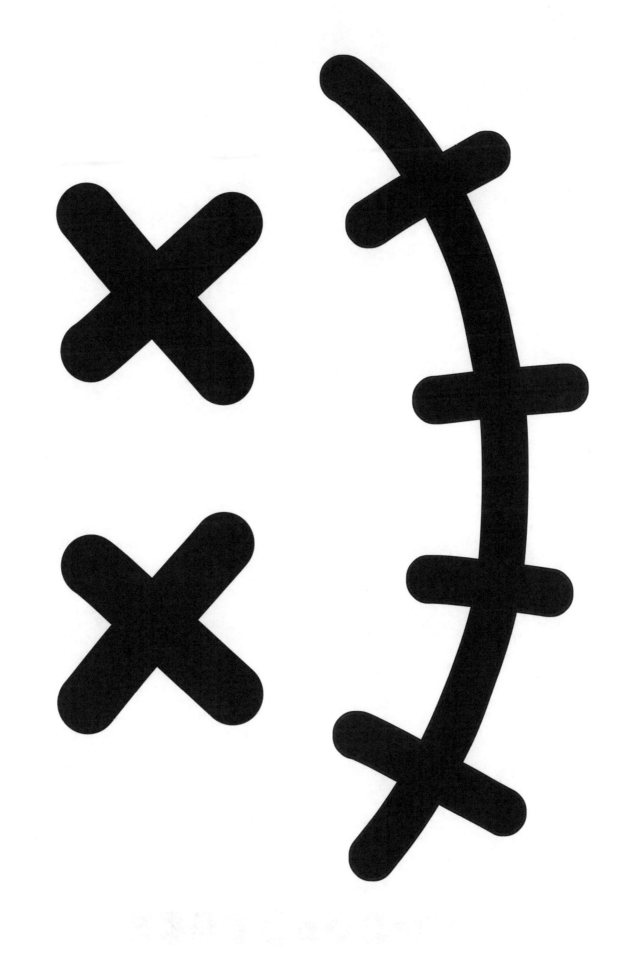

SPOOKY FACE

CUTE CAT

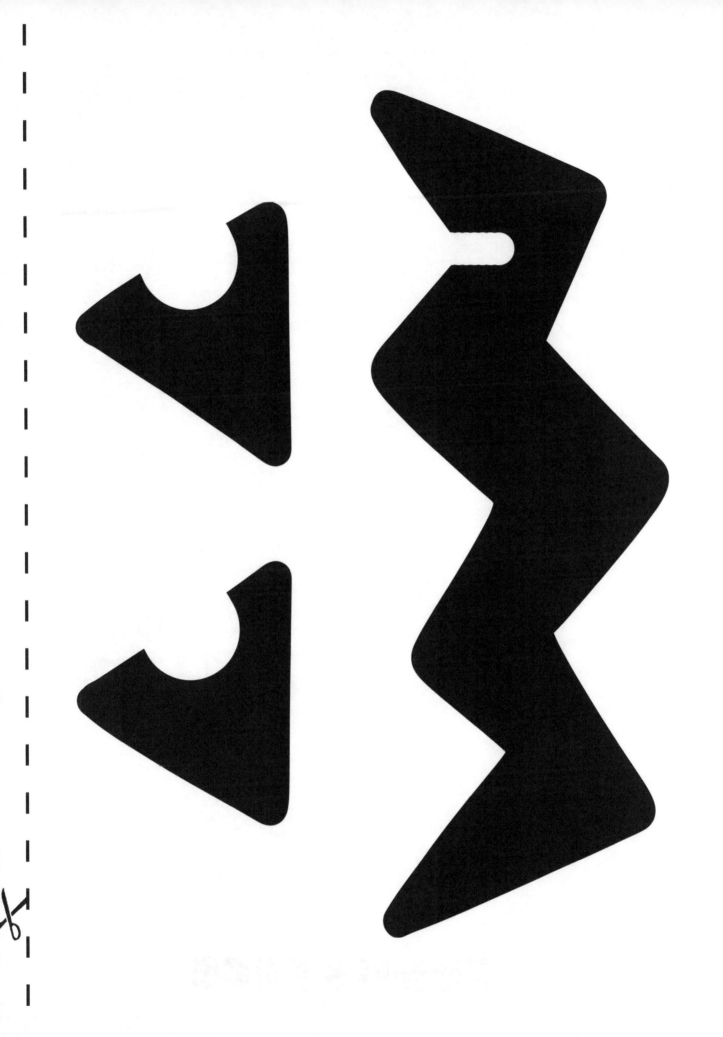

FUNNY FACE

CUTE BAT

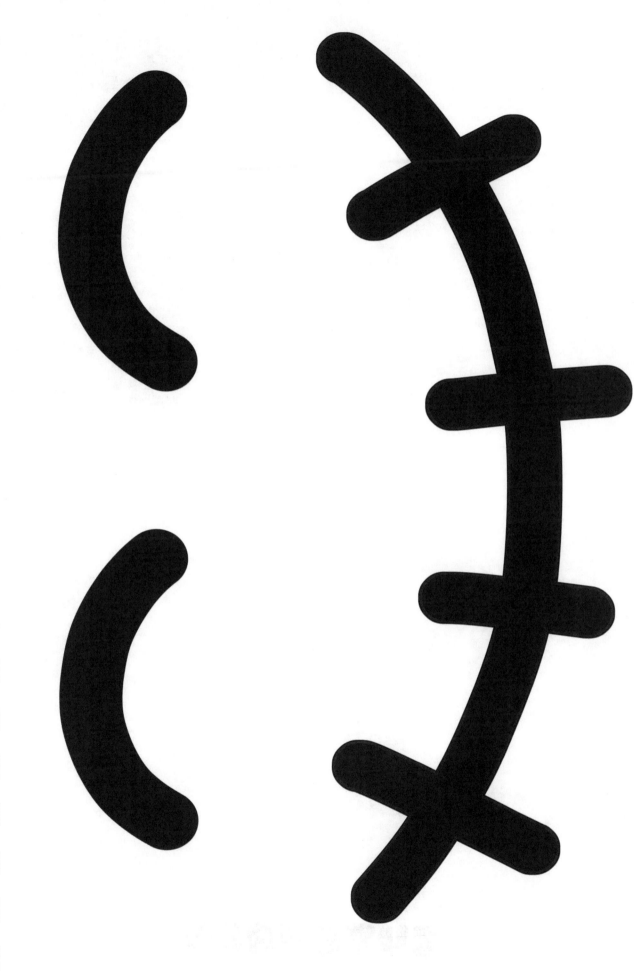

CUTE FACE

WEREWOLF FOOTPRINT

SPOOKY FACE

FRANKENSTEIN

CUTE BATS

CUTE FACE

GHOST AND STARS

SPOOKY FACE

BAT AND STARS

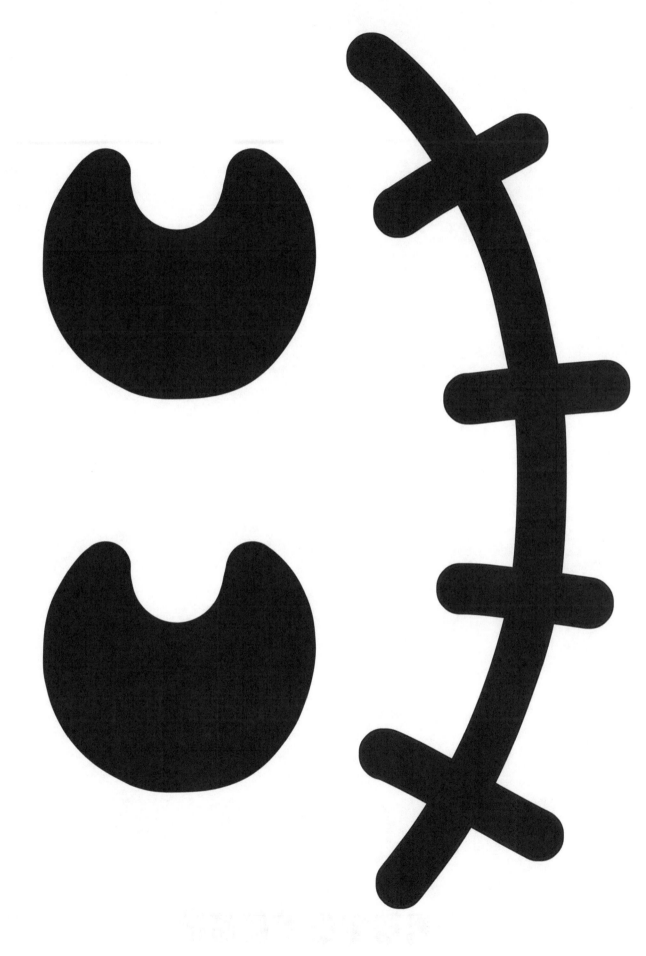

CUTE FACE

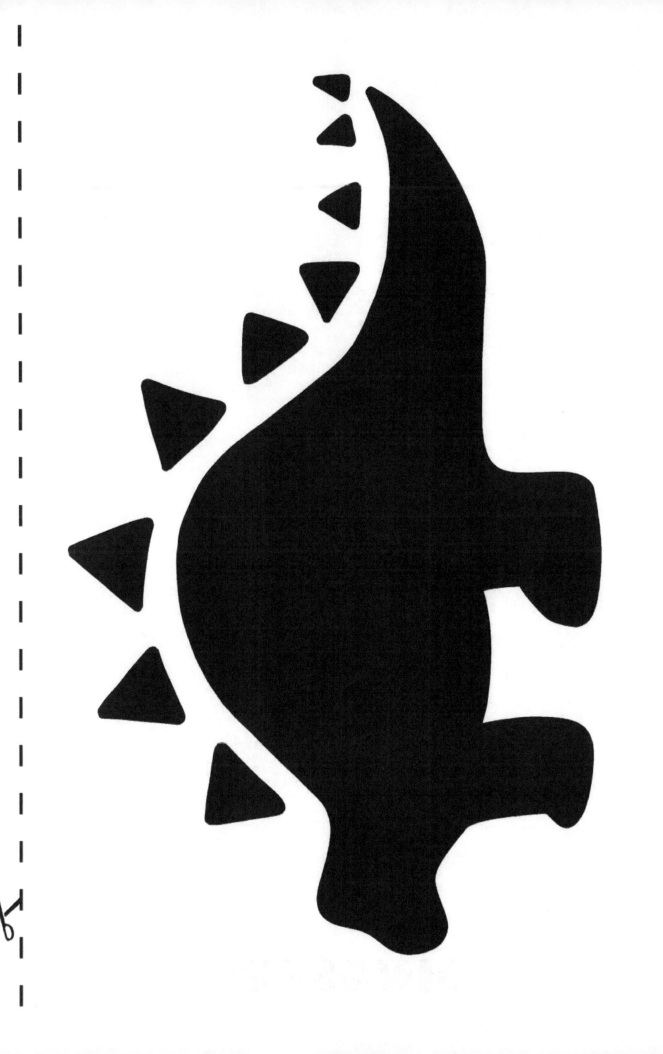

DINOSAUR

FUNNY FACE

VAMPIRE FACE

MOON AND STARS

CUTE FACE

CUTE SPIDERS

SCARY FACE

ONE-EYED MONSTER

MOUSE

boo

CUTE FACE

LOVELY FACE

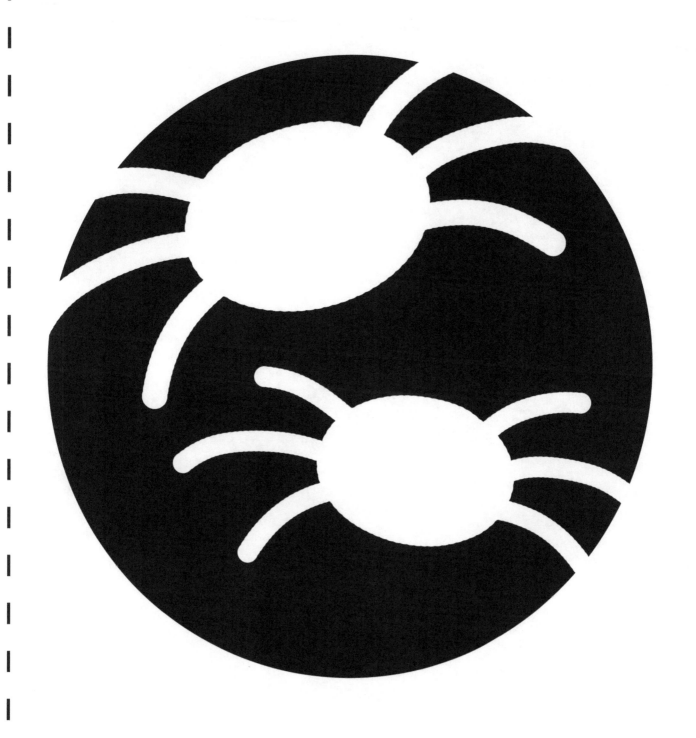

CUTE SPIDERS

SCARY FACE

SCARY FACE

HAPPY HALLOWEEN!

HAPPY HALLOWEEN!

FREE DOWNLOAD!

EMAIL ME TO GET FREE COLORING PAGE!

RICKYTHEUNICORN@YAHOO.COM

FOLLOW @RICKYTHEUNICORN
ON INSTAGRAM FOR MORE DESIGNS!

Made in United States
Troutdale, OR
10/07/2024

23502234R00060